D0493064

Contents

What is a mandir?

A **mandir** is a **Hindu** place of worship.

◀ Hindus, like Karthika and Lakchitha, go to the mandir to worship God. Some Hindus call the mandir the temple.

mandir Hindu worship God

▼ In a mandir you will see many pictures and statues of gods and goddesses. The statues are called murtis.

Many Hindus say that the gods and goddesses help them to know and love something special about God.

temple   gods   goddesses   murtis   **5**

Coming to worship

Hindu worship is called puja.

▶ When Hindus arrive in the mandir, they ring a bell to tell the murtis that they have come for puja.

◀ They put their hands together and bow their heads to greet the murtis.

puja   greet

► They give the **priest** food and **gifts** for the murtis. The priest is called a **pujari.**••••••

The priest **offers** the food and gifts to the murtis. What is he offering here?

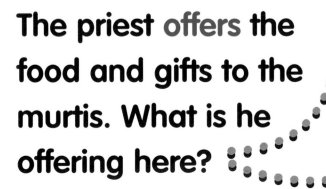

priest   **gifts**   **pujari**   **offers**   **7**

The aarti ceremony

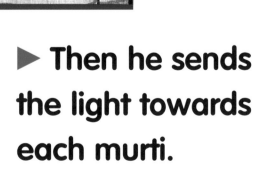

◄ The pujari offers **light** to the murtis in a **ceremony** called **aarti**. He sings and rings a bell and waves the aarti lamp in circles in front of each murti.

► Then he sends the light towards each murti.

light   **ceremony**   **aarti**

◄ **The people join in the singing.**

▶ **At the end of puja the people receive the aarti light. They move their hands over the light and over their head.**

▶ **The people also receive food called prashad.**

Hindus receive the light and the prashad as blessings from the murtis.

prashad   blessings   9

Welcome to the mandir

▼ **The pujari and his wife welcome visitors to the mandir.**

▲ **The pujari shows them the Hindu greeting. They put their hands together, bow their heads respectfully and say "Namaste".**

welcome   greeting   respectfully

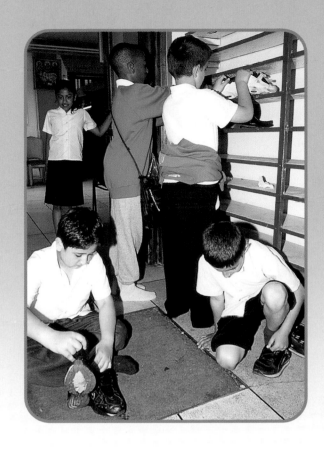

◀ Inside the mandir visitors take off their shoes. Hindus do not wear shoes in the mandir. This shows respect and keeps the carpet clean.

▶ Most Hindus who go to this mandir speak Gujarati. This Gujarati writing tells Hindus about the right way to behave.

Namaste   respect   Gujarati   11

Some favourite murtis

▼ These are the same murtis as you can see on page 5, but what is different? All the murtis are dressed each day with beautiful clothes and garlands of flowers.

Lakshman, Rama's brother

Rama

Hanuman, the monkey king

Sita, Rama's wife

garlands   Lakshman   Hanuman

Many Hindus especially love Rama and Sita. They tell exciting stories about them.

In these stories, Hanuman is Rama's devoted friend. He helped Rama to rescue Sita, when she was taken by an evil king.

▲ The murti of Hanuman always has a mace, because Hanuman used a mace to fight for Rama.

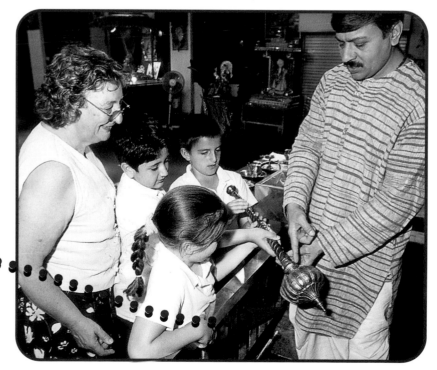

Thinking about murtis

▶ This murti is of the goddess **Durga**. She is very powerful and rides on a lion.

How many hands does she have? Can you see what she is holding in them?

Durga

▶ Esther's teacher helped her to understand why murtis have many arms. She asked Esther to draw her mum, to show everything she does to care for Esther.

▶ How many hands did Esther need to draw?

Esther's mum does not really have lots of arms, but it is a good way to show all she does. So murtis have many arms to show their special powers and all the things they do.

powers

The story of Ganesha

◀ These are murtis of Shiva and his wife Parvati.

Hindus tell this story. Parvati had a little boy called Ganesha, when Shiva was away from home. Parvati asked Ganesha to guard the door while she had a bath. Then Shiva came home and Ganesha would not let him in. Shiva was so angry that he cut off Ganesha's head.

Shiva   Parvati   Ganesha

When Parvati told Shiva that Ganesha was his son, he promised to make him better. The first head Shiva found was on an elephant, and so he used this to make a new head for Ganesha.

◀ Many Hindu children love the elephant-headed god Ganesha.

▶ Karthika showed how Hindus sometimes offer a coconut to Ganesha.

coconut

Learning about puja

People at the mandir talked to the visitors about puja.

▶ **This Hindu lady showed how the aarti light is used for puja (see pages 8 and 9).**

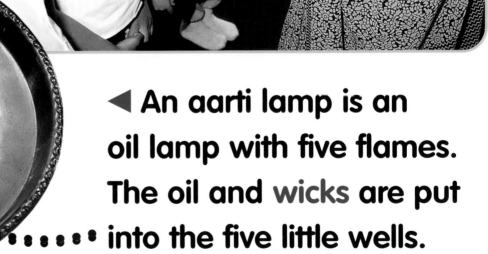

◀ **An aarti lamp is an oil lamp with five flames. The oil and wicks are put into the five little wells.**

wicks

◀ The pujari talked about sounds that Hindus listen to when they do puja. The sounds help them to feel close to God.

At the beginning and end of puja Hindus chant the sound "aum". It is written like this. •°°

◀ The visitors asked why Hindus have a coloured mark on their forehead. The pujari said it is a tilak mark, to show that they have done puja.

chant   aum   tilak

Our visit

The children enjoyed their visit to the mandir and remembered many different things.

I was happy for people to see my special place.

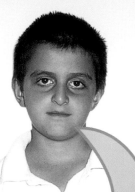

The mandir was full of statues. I liked Ganesha.

We said "Namaste" and people said it to us.

The statues wore pretty clothes and jewellery.

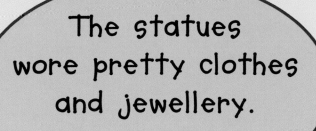

The priest showed us Hanuman's mace.

Drawing my mum helped me see why some murtis have lots of arms.

The aarti lights make people feel special.

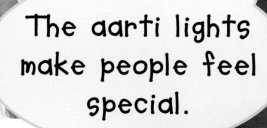

Further information for

New words introduced in the text:

aarti	Durga	greet	mace	prashad	Shiva
aum	Ganesha	greeting	mandir	priest	Sita
blessings	garlands	Gujarati	murtis	puja	temple
ceremony	gifts	Hanuman	Namaste	pujari	tilak
chant	God	Hindu	offers	Rama	welcome
coconut	goddesses	Lakshman	Parvati	respect	wicks
devoted	gods	light	powers	respectfully	worship

Background Information

Pages 4-5: Many *mandirs* in Britain are in adapted buildings rather than traditional designs. They contain shrines to various deities. They are often centres for communities that originate in areas of India or East Africa.

Hinduism is an umbrella term for religions from the Indus valley. There is great variety within Hinduism. The three main branches worship Shiva, Vishnu (with various *avatars* – incarnations – including Krishna and Rama) or Durga.

Many people find the Hindu use of images of gods and goddesses problematic. (NB the term 'idol' is offensive.) Hindus believe that the divine presence is worshipped in, or through, a variety of forms. Hindu *murtis* tell different things about the qualities and actions of God. It would be impossible to depict God in one image, but through the various 'deities' Hindus worship one God, and the stories told about these deities help Hindus to think about God. The *Rig Veda* says 'God is one but the wise call him by different names'.

Pages 6-7: *Puja* is ritual worship involving making offerings. The *murtis* are looked after, garlanded and treated as honoured guests. On page 7, the priest is offering milk.

Pages 8-9: The *aarti* ceremony, which is performed at set times in the day, is a multisensory experience. There is bell-ringing, chanting and singing. Food, water, incense, flowers, the sounds of a bell and conch shell, and light are offered to the *murtis*. Worshippers then receive the light and food (*prashad*) as from the *murtis*. It is acceptable for school visitors to observe this ceremony, but teachers should ensure that inappropriate participation, including eating *prashad*, is tactfully avoided.

Pages 10-11: '*Namaste*' is pronounced with short 'a's as in 'nana' followed by 'steh'. It is used in greetings and goodbyes. It is said originally to mean 'I salute the god in you' and reflects the Hindu belief in *atman*, the divine spirit in all living things. The gesture is the same as in greeting the *murtis* (page 6).

Pages 12-13: Stories about Rama are in the epic *Ramayana*. Rama and Sita are regarded as the ideal man and woman. The story of their exile along with Lakshman, the capture and rescue of Sita, and their triumphant return to Ayodhya, is retold each year, culminating in the Diwali festival. Hanuman is worshipped as the ideal of loyalty and devoted service.

Pages 14-15: Durga is also known as Kali. She is quite fierce. Her eight arms hold the weapons and emblems given to her by other

Parents and Teachers

gods to help overcome the demon of chaos. The gestures, body, hand and face markings, items carried, clothing, and animal 'vehicles' of the various deities all symbolise aspects of their powers, or actions in the stories about them.

Pages 16-17: Shiva is one of the main gods in Hindu worship. Parvati is worshipped in various forms including Durga. Ganesha, the 'remover of obstacles', is often worshipped at the beginning of *pujas* and of new undertakings. He is depicted with a broken tusk, a fat belly held by a snake belt, and riding a rat. The story that these signify can be investigated.

Pages 18-19: A *tilak* mark is a sign of a person belonging to the Hindu religion, or of having done *puja*. It is applied differently by different Hindu sects and sub-sects (e.g. as a 'U' by worshippers of Vishnu and as three horizontal lines by worshippers of Shiva). A red dot sticker, sometimes called a *bindi*, is traditionally worn by married women, and cosmetic versions are fashion accessories with girls.

Suggested Activities

Show pictures of a range of *mandir* buildings and discuss what makes them *mandirs* (use/design?).

Visit a local *mandir* or use a virtual visit. Discuss how it made the children feel.

Invite a Hindu to tell how they do *puja* and what their religion means to them.

Make garlands to honour a visitor/teacher. Say '*Namaste*' at register time.

Show and discuss an *aarti* tray and paraphernalia, but avoid inappropriate role-play of *puja*.

Read stories of the gods and goddesses and relate these to the images.

Books and Websites

Hindu Artefacts Teaching Pack, Vida Barnett, Articles of Faith, 1995

My Hindu Faith (Big Book), Anita Ganeri, Evans, 1998

RE 'gateway' sites provide recommendations for videos and books and links to organisations, sources of artefacts and other useful websites for teachers and pupils.
http://www.theresite.org.uk – 27 links to KS1 sites on Hinduism and to virtual tours of *mandirs*
http://re-xs.ucsm.ac.uk – links to introductory sites on Hinduism
http://theredirectory.org.uk – links to Hindu organisations
http://www.iskcon.org.uk – resources from the Hare Krishna movement
http://www.hindunet.org/hindu_pictures/GodandGoddesses/god.shtml

■ Draw images of some of the gods and goddesses and investigate the symbols associated with them.

■ Let children draw someone who cares for them to show all their qualities and what they do. Identify the activities that Esther (page 15) has depicted (e.g. she gives me a tissue when I cry).

■ Act a circle song telling the Rama and Sita story, to the tune of and beginning: 'There was a princess long ago'. (And Rama was a handsome prince/They went to live in the forest green/A lovely deer came running by/Ravana took Sita away/The monkeys came and rescued her/Everyone is happy now.) For more details, see: http://homepage.ntlworld.com/jeanmead/re

■ Find images of Ganesha on Hindu cards and wedding invitations.

Index